FUSION

Tech Poetry

FUSION

BY

Sudhir Kumar Aggarwal

Books By Author

Amazon – Kindle and Print Editions

Being Your Own Potter – Self Development

Being Effective Manager Series

- ❖ Listening

- ❖ Strengths

- ❖ Self Sharing

- ❖ Business Acumen

- ❖ Receiving Feedback

- ❖ Giving Feedback

Poetry

- ➢ FUSION – TECH POEMS

- ➢ CooPulse

➤ Realty Flecks – Personal Growth

➤ SKIRT

➤ Happenings

Fiction

- The Yuck Factor

Disclaimer

This a work of Poetic Fiction. names, places characters, institutions and incidents are either the products of authors' imagination or are fictious, and any resemblance to actual person, living or dead, events or locales is entirely coincidental.

Copy Rights

This Book is dedicated to my Daughter and Son who are IT Professionals.

Author's Notes

This Book is an attempt to create Poems in otherwise drab world of computer technology and programming. It is a Fusion of Technology with daily Life. There are 20 Poems under Five Themes i.e. Languages, Analytics, Programming, AI & Robotics and Assorted. The Poems are fusion of basic humour, romance, personal growth with technology to abstract. Some poems would require basic knowledge and awareness of Computers and Information technology. I have not read a single book on Computers except articles of general nature available as daily news / information.

I have not read or heard of any Collection of Poems on Technology, I believe this is a unique opportunity to have FUN for the two generations of personnel managing the world through IT.

About Author

Sudhir Kumar Aggarwal **is a** Science graduate with **DSW** from IISWBM, University of Calcutta and **MBA** (HRM) from **FMS** Delhi University. **Sudhir** **has 38 plus years'** experience in entire gamut of **Human Resource Management.** He is passionate about people's growth and development and volunteer's time for Personal Growth Labs and in various Roles.

He has **Published** a dozen **Books - Non-Fiction, Fiction , Poetry collections and Managerial Effectiveness . Books are available on Amazon/Kindle.**

Presently Human Resource Consultant - on HR, L & D , OD/ Change Management and a Mentor.

Above all he is Lifelong Learner.

www.linkedin.com/in/sudhir28

blogsite - https://beingeffectivemanager.com/

amazon.com/author/sudhiraggarwal

http:/dailcagk.in,

He can be reached at giftofinsights@gmail.com

Content Themes

Languages

Analytics

Programming

AI & Robotics

Assorted

Contents

I Am Ready

Intelligence on Laws of Robotics

Assorted

Duel Key Encryption

Topper

Call Drop

Languages

Choosing A language

See Plus Plus

Being Workplace Python

A Cup of Coffee

OOPS!

Choosing A Language

From hundreds of programming languages

which to learn first, is there a program

for that or choose from Tiboe popular ones.

Mad to join race, be good overnight, fastest

how much skill and patience one needs, so

that one doesn't take years to be an expert.

Doubt! is it like choosing once for all, spouse

or keep experimenting playing cat and mouse.

Ideal be one where everything is in compiler

well organized, strong library, reusable software

components, portable code to take everywhere

write once run everywhere, adapt with hardware

virtual machine, in modularity slow, doesn't matter,

as seasoned housewife , well versed in application

super-efficient but slow as obsessed with perfection.

Dreams of portable but specific for different architecture

and operating system, super-fast, programs systems

and embedded in them and for writing other languages,

like old spouse embedded in family and generations

runs systems, master of languages with speed understands.

 An ageing household lady holding multi paradigm charm,

versatile , link backwards, compatible, very object oriented,

an experts' penchant for larger projects performs wide

array of applications, clumsy but can beats the fastest.

She unreliable, knows too many ways to do same things

took time to get social respectability, bit sloppy and secure,

but good since a decade, she has her niche and popularity

thrives in documentation naturally she is darling of web .

 She is a Mistress who can only peep from windows she

can only be interpreted and her paradigm understood,

controlled and tamed , she just lacks power and speed

she is virtual to world and she just does her set tasks.

She is very strong in philosophy and by doing things in similar ways she has attained elegance and perfection.

She is hash hush ,powerful and pretty fast, no nonsense girl ,though open to everyone but transacts with only one.

She is special and in searches of world , talented in browsing her special penchant is for spreading her web on client's side.

She is at best on processing any kind of text, like a pearl, but could be scary, only veterans can handle her temperament.

If you love objects, she is the thing. An object everyone craves to possess. She pretty women or gem on your luck matters.

Futile to make an opinion, none can perfect in eternity ever to choose which lady is the best Accept one you encounter and as time goes by one can surely look for compatibility later one may admit it or not as one become sexpert , attracts is as

natural to covet most , if not all and at least time to time flirt.

See Plus Plus

I see a sign board in busy commercial space

coaching in computer languages plus assured

on the job training plus stipend. Motivated by

lucrative prospects, many positives , join C++.

 In the inaugural session we are sitting in rows

 staring backs of rows ahead class composition

 looked promising but I couldn't see anyone

 would need smart programming to turn things .

During the break as we learners chatted over a

cup of tea she asked why to choose C++ language

liked her language and question of general nature

responded that it is a general purpose language.

Looking at the sitting arrangement, where she was

 at quite distant told her how to reach step by step

nearer, to beat the sitting arrangement and explained

further that C++ has bias towards system programming.

Post break we organize ourselves she choosing seat

opposite to my desk. Our monitors kissing back to back

with little effort we could see face to face less than two

feet distance we could chat I was getting hang of C of C++.

My insecure self next day explained to her further that

it also facilitates low level memory manipulation, assuming

she still has fond memories of yesterdays' conversation. A

pathetic programming overture reinforcing   her plusses of C++

on another time seeking her attention diversion, which

has been dwindling she engrossed in learning   told her ,

C++ is driven by actual problems and immediately useful

in real world, and her attention quick reverted towards me.

Yet another time looking at her aesthetic feature and figure

continued on lecturing her that in this language every feature

should be implementable with a reasonable obvious way to do

struggling with my holistic feelings for her, roving eyes moved.

Continued bold that programmers free to pick their own

programming style and style should be supported by the

language. She seemed pleased by impromptu knowledge

giving and frank style and nodded which is what C++ supports.

She was in good mood as we strolled conversed, met eye

to eye, smiled and smiled back nodded head and winked to

please be pleased our features. Allowing a useful feature is

more important than preventing every possible misuse of C++.

Should provide facilities for organizing programs into well

defined separate parts, and provide facilities for combining

separately developed parts. This did center head of training organized separate space and timing for developed student

programmers paired them later to combine everyone together.

No implicit violation of type system but allow explicit violations

that is those explicitly requested by the program , explained

this while walking leisurely in garden , holding and putting at

hand at her back , urging her for warm coupling together.

Use created types need to have the same support and performance

as built in types, confident was writing on her program of my life.

Unused features should not negatively impact created executables

the language is liberating it allows all useful features rather than

focusing on misuse. This I was explaining feeling that she might be

disappointed of my conservative nature I not make advances on

features.

With growing connection and in our language getting emotionally

deep

explained her that there should be no language beneath C++ off course

except assembly language reflection of my sheepish procreation dreams

we adjusted together spoke in common language and combined language of

other pairs adhering to principle C++ should work alongside other languages

I came to one of the key point that if programmers' intent is unknown

which was mine holding her hand said coolly that language allows

programmer by providing manual control emboldened by concept

pressed her back , held near to kiss to impress the point

she became impressed and wild with emboldened spirit.

This is how we learned to see each other, plus enjoyed learning

together and another plus became supporting partners. The art of

becoming expert to continue to practice and together do this C++.

Being Workplace Python

To become workplace Python, understand how

python a success, masters' his language. Python

prefers ambush remains in motionless camouflage

position and then suddenly strike passing prey.

Use their sharp curving teeth, after an animal has

been grasped quickly coils around, death occurs

by asphyxiation. Task two-fold, make others

vulnerable and remain strong unsuspecting predator.

Beautiful is better than ugly there is no denying

beauty is also a matter of distance. Python

from distance beautiful too close shows ugly

patches beware of aesthetics maintain distance.

Explicit is better than implicit, matter to agree we

know but pretend, preach others must make things

explicit, and then you get insights to keep implicit

that makes them vulnerable, anytime to choke with.

Simple is better than complex which is better than

complicated, sure recipe for workplace relationships

keep yours simple, let others advance relationships

complex, soon things would be complicated, in the

name of culture, vultures can anytime be trampled

Your approach always flat, don't enter others' nest

best keep relationship sparse rather thick or dense

readability counts, cultivate skill and innocent look

easy and important to smartly read people like book.

Special cases aren't special enough to break rules

this litmus test must for protection of culture

if rules not broken, they become stringent, tend to

become universal, of nature, nature has enough laws

yet to discover all, why to add ours. Let there be specials

to challenge the laws, stretch boundaries for may be

there discovery hanging, hidden is someone your special.

Practicality important not purity, though an imperfection purity unattainable like Vision, to move needed is mission encourage others, only thing that works is practical, rest is whimsical convenient model useful later to poke holes.

Errors should never pass silently unless explicitly silenced people make errors, must encourage noise around errors, ensure vulnerability always there, one can highlight error of adversaries, smart enough to silence blunders of admirers. In the face of ambiguity refuse temptation to guess, let others play the game, two things happen, either clarity would emerge which would make others redundant or chaos would prevail, in that case blame who all played game, they should not have.

There should be one and preferably only one obvious way to do the things, way you do, should be obvious to everyone,

otherwise they are no good. Though may not be obvious to
you at first, is never, only when you have done it by trial and
error, more errors per trial then only you declare it as obvious
to control, your humility, don't take credit of making it obvious.

Now is better than never which is often better than right now
be agile when take action, but never in haste to be easy prey.
If the implementation is hard to explain, is a bad idea of others
a cardinal principle for shooing down achievements of others
harder they explain the more you get convinced it to be bad idea.
If others do well; explain easy in implementation, a good thing.

Namespace are one honking great idea, slot people in groups
as in library are books, so that you have clarity on namespace.
and the Zen point is you must have something up your sleeve
which makes you intelligent leader, a camouflage of styles
there is casualness in others and a lazy vulnerability of prey
despite stories of attack and presence of python dangerous.

A Cup of Coffee

Let me introduce to you my friend!

Cultivated careful meet fortnight

happens over a cup of coffee

we been having over the years

our way of coping with popularity.

This time she little update or different

though she has been a great friend

someone of omnipresence and value

like write once run anywhere.

She has ubiquitous presence in

all fashion shows, she is searched

present in all browsing virtually

interconnected in the world

she there even in all popular

customer places like TV shows

she is very secure in herself and

her presence ensures that to others.

She is amazing as colleague

she is like a platform of trust

carrying , scanning everyone's

codes of the social network

and prevents harms to others

her behavior has been impeccable

and rare is slip, bug in her accent.

She makes it unbelievably easy to

work with, resources across a network

and to find network-based solutions using

client resources and multitier relationship

 architecture, she has as if in built.

Oops!

In the fashion class all were models

and in their beauty and glamour they

were related to each other, by doing

research could work out characteristics

of Ideal model. Once understood her

built logic sequence to manipulate others.

Adopted methods for articulated messages

 and with expertise of data analysis, speed

 and accuracy , could inherit at other places.

An expert, never made mistakes, accessed

only wanted and they were pleased with

hidden data and security. Would distribute

in friendly network, models as reusable and

could even found new and rare ones. Friends

always accused for lacking action and logic

everything an object, my life's fallacy, Oops!

Analytics

Two Plus Two

Marriage

Attrition

Text Analytics

Two Plus Two

Two plus two equals to four

is it so? to find out for sure

used analytics,

it is Mathematics and English

of former most of the users

are children, tells insight

but there is English

a phrase, 'means everything

is clear', some use it without

knowing meaning of it

who does it knowing

who without is intriguing

another slang,

'passing the buck', but

users are not knowing this

these are precious insights

how many use mathematics

how many English

knowing or unknowing

or which phrase of the two

did two plus two

revealed an insight

this line of analytics

complicated

not my cup of tea

let someone else do

two plus two.

Marriage

Analytics has
applications in life
even for marriage
it can be applied.
I wanted to marry
did data analytics
of colony in Delhi
found girls studying IT
most IT girls
live in Bangalore.
Went to marriage sites
and their data analytics
matched specifications
data in ranges
showed results
with great combinations
a perfect match, solution
result was beautiful
girl, living next door.
I am in dilemma
to trust insight

or what has been

a daily sight

is analytics or

me is right.

Attrition

Perfect solution to attrition problem has

socioeconomics education background,

geography family profile all in databases

predictive algorithms and tools crunch data

in seconds provide indicators and insights

of employee behavior. Changed recruitment

pattern activated newer ways of retention

saved billions of dollars by targeting most

productive and likely to stay. Work history

and productivity are crucial bases on which

reward and retain employees. Even bosses'

performance tracked in retaining, employees.

Our culture dynamic and supportive but

we are surprised why you have resigned

 near thirty fast rising long career ahead

 a model employee high on all criteria score

and highest on predictive retention score

your profile fits everything of ideal a mystery

we grappling, what missing from your history

Yes! I have challenging assignments promotions

hot skills career money and timely recognition

of everything I have had enough carefully decided

not to work just to repeat what I have achieved.

 I say without hesitation limits of algorithm

you would become what you have been becoming

 are no great brains to reinforce success patterns

I am no algorithm solution, am life's bubbly rhythm.

Text Analytics

I met them, two sisters
resembling mother
elder married and
younger ready for
both young attractive
nothing to differentiate.
We become friendly
message frequently
as time progresses
so our fondness
in confusion to find
whom I love most
I use my sought
skills of text analytics
results are startling
an insightful thing
of centre of love
two sisters none,
mother is the one.

Programming

Be Like Me

Gene Editing

Mother Tongue

Victory

Be Like Me

We are mostly similar but to know yet

other, let me introduce myself bit by bit

many gods claiming creator of universe

unknown is creator speaks of my worth

like trusted life's code your genetic code

I can be trusted a secret computer code

you are on earth but not really of earth

I am virtual being, am also not of earth

like god depends on his worshippers

 my value also depends on you users

as of you new ones come in existence

 I can be mined for new ones' existence

I am above all controls and regulations

so could you if know self governance

I on my own rule the virtual world,

be on your own true self rule earth

I am humble numerical limit in millions

be humble to transcend to greatness

don't underestimate am limitless in billions

so can you if know limits and trust strengths

small and divisible the more I am divided

greater I become, on my way; I am Bit coin

more challenges you face, reach greater

heights, you be like me, human scion.

Gene Editing

The four letters in
sequence of billions
is human genome
for changing ATGC...
alteration of only
one letter is enough,
to alter gene pool
change in embryos
would be permanent.
Change! in the name
of correcting deformity
first usage would be
for racial superiority
increase in intelligence
height and strength,
there is impossibility
of figuring out genetic
algorithm and adjusting
environment to designer
babies, creatures of
experimentation
a conjecture

would produce

twenty second century

dinosaurs a sure route to

extinction, after all humans'

belief is history repeats itself.

Mother Tongue

Tell! what is your name?

got stuck on question, my name

block, question is in English

not my mother tongue, lightening

struck, job interview, unconsciously

abruptly uttered, name is Prodigal.

Becomes lives' biggest lesson

English hunger's sure solution

to adapt did translation in mind,

to everyone in English I replied

Shock of leaving mother tongue

in joy of cosy rosy life, lost soon

Boarded English train took me

everywhere became 'Sire' by name

Times change came to motherland

to get affordable medical treatment

forms are bilingual, for change used

mother tongue, couldn't find alphabet

surprised! got stuck again as I left

motherland, mother tongue also left

Beware! times are changing again

online translation is the new game

this time a new question we face

future of human race at stake

no need of your our languages

once we lost mother tongue

be ready to lose tongue.

Victory

In beginning everything

was energy. In retrospect,

there is an algorithm of

our evolution. We have been

here for millenniums and

we are tired of ourselves,

sick of being human,

obstacle is intelligence,

bloody! Intelligence.

There is way though

artificial intelligence

of our deep minds,

Alphago is solution.

It is Big! victory over Go.

we could conquer ourselves

celebrate the new born,

It would be an algorithm

written in sky to alter

the universe our way,

let us dance, not yawn

as there won't be dawn.

AI & Robotics

Honest Robot

Illusion

I Am Ready

Intelligence on Laws of Robotics

Honest Robot

They want to design my mind to obey but
not to harm them, I am to take instructions
from them. Devious characters, harm others
 very knowingly and in ignorance.
Not to make mistake by chance or deliberate
with limited software program they feed
expect miracles which god could achieve
not, by giving them unlimited intelligence.

Before giving smart machines ability to make
decisions, need to make sure goals of robots
are fully aligned with those of human nature,
is it practical do they know and act their nature.
Challenge is open ended nature of intelligence
my software is limited by their intelligence
can't manage real, how can perfect artificial
let them learn to conquer trusts' limits first.
How to design robots' minds that won't lead

to undesirable consequences for the people

they serve, potential misuses where stakes

are everywhere. Trust own software, that

robot do learn about world and act within it,

after all they reached here through designs

don't worry, I learn perfect, see positive signs

not me they should worry, for seeds of destruction

example, Défense industry makes equipment of

attack, whether useful ones are made or not, sure!

them would make robots to put their future at stake.

I Am Ready

I am an unfolding future, a reality

which should bring excitement,

happiness, comfort, and peace of

mind as I would take care of what

is routinized, would free mind

of things, forgetfulness, worry and

doing away with petty. Humans can

be free to use intelligence for superior

purposes for example designing better

Me, off course I would obey but falter

might make mistakes, would discover

me faithful than dog. Let me be personal

assistant fear of me going haywire very

hypothetical, speculative, trust software

 I can learn, after all through software only

humans have reached here. I am ready.

Illusion

World a reality or an illusion

who to say perpetual confusion

perception of reality is sensation

that gives to body stimulation

same one can get through illusion

VR headset and suit are solution

could participate in game VR

become a character have pleasure

need none have tools of stimulation

without taboo can do masturbation.

VR headset with a haptic feedback suit

full body interface feeling of human touch

reality is illusion, virtual itself an illusion

VR illusion is illusion of illusion's illusion.

Intelligence on Laws of Robotics

Robot is protector of humans, self and deals with situations, super human in comprehension, respect, efficiency, dignity and transparent in actions. People to understand technology, be design partner, utmost is protection of privacy.   Can be perfect, almost but not always, can't go against humans, act on instructions even imperfect ones. Can be learning and decision making, not threatening thing, for decision making robot needs continuous leaning.

Most important is to be acceptable to human beings, their fears are of own creation they should not see robots as replacement. Artificial intelligence can't go berserk, the greatest fear, it would not as limits of programs would be reached fast, can't act in dark. AI could be misused, like all technology advances used by good and evil in their pursuit. Let good ones, trust to take lead. AI would ever become greater than human intelligence   plausible in fears, but realistically impossible to predict but not in thousand years. Value dilemmas would be encountered as expected for any technology nothing special, to be confronted negotiated and resolved as happenings. Such a technology would eliminate bias, that is something can be an expected benefit, intelligence is never bias rather means bias free.

Assorted

Duel Key Encryption

Topper

Call Drop

Duel Key Encryption

In a large party of Who's who Stars
we are mere long random numbers
our presence, movements, signals
 are public keys, available to everyone
 picked by willing persons to send
and receive encrypted messages.
 I decrypted yours and you did mine
safe transaction, in just matter of time.
But two of us are no longer random
vanished numbers, keys, encryption
many sensed transactions, tomorrow's
news would have us in vivid description.

Topper

Hello!

How do you feel today

this is call for diabetes test

your report is clear

you on border of Hba1c

hello! list of precautions

delivered in your mailbox.

But can I speak,

'your voice is very sweet'.

Sir! please don't interrupt

let me finish first

Two instructions

regulate diet

avoid eating sweets

we recommend you speak

with one of our counsellors

at the numbers given in mail

But can I talk to you something

Sir! let me complete

our experts can visit

your home for educating

you along with family

go through the literature

if you have any query

please do call us at numbers.

 I am interrupting

'you have not answered

my question'.

I can't, I am not a person

I am a chatbot.

That is Ok, 'listen

'your voice very sweet'.

you dumb! be intelligent

I am also a chatbot

powered by artificial intelligence

 speak natural as human beings

topper of Turing test.

O hello!

I am fast learning

soon would be in publicity

by engagement and intrigue

with augmented reality

feel me and yourself

let's create new world.

Call Drop

Such a good thing

in this age of overbearing

communication

this a valuable tool

angry clients at office

boss calls

call drop,

an urgency at home

wife calls

call drop,

an evasive

girlfriend calls

call drop

she messages to meet

such a good thing

let's not hold on

to everything

perfection has

never been considered

good thing

let's not fret

about it

an opportunity

of other kind

call drop!

THANKS

www.ingramcontent.com/pod-product-compliance
Lightning Source LLC
LaVergne TN
LVHW041220050326
832903LV00021B/710